Trouble Sleeping

TROUBLE SLEEPING

PHIL HALL

Ph.

April 23/05

Brick Books

CANADIAN CATALOGUING IN PUBLICATION DATA

Hall, Phil, 1953–
Trouble sleeping

Poems.
ISBN 0-894078-11-X

I. Title.

PS8565.A449T76 2000   C811'.54   C00-931615-9
PR9199.3.H34T76 2000

We acknowledge the support of the Canada Council for the Arts
for our publishing programme. The support of the Ontario Arts
Council is also gratefully acknowledged.

Sections here have appeared in *The Capilano Review* and *Our Times*.

Typeset in Minion. The stock is acid-free Zephyr Antique laid.
Printed and bound by The Porcupine's Quill Inc.

Brick Books
431 Boler Road, Box 20081
London, Ontario N6K 4G6

brick.books@sympatico.ca

This *haibun*
(a Japanese form of interwoven journey-prose and poetry)
is for my children, my sisters, and Ann.

* * *

With special thanks to Martha, and Chris.

NOT THE ELMS I want back
but the blue-green lustre
    of the bug that killed them –
its metal sheen an armour
    encasing Mom's heart

not that fist of engine block
    the tractor winched out by chain
but the slight sway of its weight
    in the dying elm – a rare give
to Dad's rage

    not our silver mailbox – its cable
absorbed into the growing trunk –
    that swallowed choke – that ring scar's
box caught the only response
    to my rescue hopes – starling straw
starling straw

    not those sick elms I want back
but that nest of correspondences –
    the anchor-fruit & the bright seed
(the rancour-fruit & the blight-seed)
    of the deaths I honour
that were without honour

'I'M SO THIRSTY I could drink a cow flat!'

A line. Not mine. A childhood. Not mine. A summer. I am thinking

of. Right now. Startled upright. In bed, a noise – what?

Again? I am that thirsty. In a shaken disillusioned way. I am that flat

cow. Scared, scarred hide. Hiding. Parched cringe.

The usual room is here. And its butchery endeavours: touch my

past and instead of one story, normal cow, nourishment – no, it falls

apart into wrapped steaks. And the wrapped steaks – crawl. On the

desk, little putrid written-bits.

ON SEA-LEGS of butterfat
toddlers wander mountain trails

their fathers' heads slung on their backs
bent drybrush winds

a father's eyes open – blinking
elevation wettens – obscures

against pupils – crystals
opening their little arms compass-wide

a head with its dated pencil-mustache
whispering to its climbing child

once an air-foothold held
as air billows from the mouth of the child

to offer the same advice to the trail
helpless head along for the climb

to the ice cave where a garden glove
has been left gripping a turd at the mouth

white air too high to not be snow
too ground-close to be said to fall

powder mustache
handrift

IF ONLY I HADN'T been forced to swallow a teaspoon of my own urine, hadn't dropped my jam knife on the floor for the dogs to lick, hadn't sung *Old Dan Tucker* at the supper table ('washed his face in a frying pan / combed his hair with a wagon-wheel / died with a toothache in his heel'). Then I would have been able to stay home sick with the 'hooping cough and watch afternoon movies with my mother. I would have cried before bed, but I might have been rescued by dark, official strangers.

Instead, my body still feeds on what it needs to get rid of. My knives, too, feed on themselves, still eat their own droppings. There are never any new players, no new versions of the past. No child survives.

I am a fundamentalist when it comes to my version, this sacred text, this recipe for blame as flight-fuel, this remedy for home.

CEASELESS ORBITS
the illusion of stillness
    hoop-dance in boardroom table
festation's implacable
    knotted whorls let
dubious voraciousness
    tempt crucial absurdities

stigma ovary water fog ease Siam

    the battle of the little
rivulet &
    big isosceles licked
pitless in the torting range
    sick of cautious perfection
let silk cosset bared grounds there
    are no slow ones

stigma ovary water fog ease Siam

    grey marble & ocean froth
these relentless attempts at
    keeping circles that never
quite break or get completed
    wedding ring in the toy box
this wolfcup my son gave me
    this wounded wolf-heart from Dad

stigma ovary water fog ease Siam

    (R. Buckminster
Fuller sees his dome in near-
    bubbles in a ship's wake &
Ernest Thomas
    Seton covers traps with snow
in an H-shape
    but Lobo halts between that

stigma ovary water fog ease Siam

 H-trap's horns – stops short of the
jaws of the zygal – backs out)
 I sip coffee – *nothing* is
going on – in heap's clothing
 in marble green ocean froth
in Ulterior Thule
 in transitu

ROKEBY WASN'T an actual village, more the top end of Bobcaygeon, a place-to-be-nearly-from, a road-fork where the eventual by-pass would begin or end, depending. Mostly there was Rokeby Lumber with its red outbuildings and Fargo trucks converted to drive backwards as forklifts, Anderson Brother's Grocery & Gas, the Galway and Buckhorn Roads branching north.

Out Buckhorn Road, by the dump, a sign said BANCROFT 63 MILES. Stop by that sign and look right, most of the year, you'd see Herb Nichols in a lawn chair among the knobby sumac, ruminating on the fortunes and duties of Dump Manager. Or he'd be setting fire to the gull-cliff at dusk, then sauntering into town along the shoulder of the highway. On one arm he might be wearing a charred commode lid.

Entering Rokeby, Herb had to pass first a little war-time bungalow of tarred sprinkle-brick that stood in the wedge where the town-line intersected the Galway Road. Following the town-line, he would pass fields of government trees doing poorly, the home of the Hydro Co. representative, Verulam Cemetery, the Township Sheds. Then he'd be at the other top entry-road to the town, where the other lumber yard, Jermyn's, was also whining down for the night.

In that first bungalow, at the town-line, lived an old man my father had befriended, becoming a sort of surrogate son because the man's actual son was never around. Most of the time no one knew where the son even was.

The son's father, by this time, was a wet-eyed, white-haired (lots of it, swept back off a high brow) widower, portly but demure, who looked like a European diplomat in hiding, an ex-Nazi or small Tzar. He seemed overly apologetic about something that had lost its specifics long ago. His breathing came with effort; he was quiet, clean shaven, neater than most. His silence filled the car with gratitude on those afternoons when my father took us for drives along the sideroads near the farmhouse we rented.

From the back seat I'd watch for empties. My father would pass a pup of rye to the old man. A 22 rifle would be loaded between them, safety off, in case a partridge or rabbit flared. When bottles glinted, I'd be let out to fetch and then position those bottles on fence rails. The old man never tried shooting, but watched the entertainment, eyes sparkling, as my father and I took turns. Neither did he ever unbutton his trousers expansively and piss, along with my father, onto a crushed carcass of porcupine while singing that Hank Locklin song: *send me the pillow that you dream on / so darlin' I can dream on it too.* I was grateful to the old man for such discretions; I snuck off among the purple trilliums when I needed to.

I was a good shot, but I wore glasses. The rims were black on top and clear underneath. My father thought that having to wear glasses was a character flaw. He still had 20/20 vision, and reminded me each time we went to the dump to scrounge and shoot rats. I'd throw his emptied bottle into the air, he'd shoot it and Herb Nichols would laugh.

Actually, I liked to miss. I loved to listen to the bullet go on sounding through leaves, or to what I imagined was the bullet going on sounding through leaves, but was probably only the silence of the aftermath, the woods noises that were always there, unnoticed until the crack. The only other time I ever heard such deep sounds was when I was hidden by saplings and purple trilliums, relieving myself, studying my own scat, just listening.

bullrod (my word for everything then)

THE OLD MAN'S SON'S NAME was Cec. Cecil, his father called him, but no one else ever did. My father, when we were out of the house, always called the son 'that prick' or 'that crazy prick.' The odd thing is: my father's name was also Cec.

Cec and Cec, they used to be, the two Cec's. When you saw the two Cec's coming – look out!

'Have you ever tried holding onto grass with your shoulder blades so you won't fall off the planet?' The Cec's were apparently good at that, or came to be.

Crudities and confusions were alluded to, and sometimes they returned, for instance in black and white photographs that had been folded many times and crammed into the back of our First Aid Kit. I turned one photograph upsidedown to assure myself that the nude woman in it was not my mother bent over, laughing at night beside a Packard.

The bad Cec's father's name was Alistair. I think old Alistair would have loved to transpose his parental disappointments more fully by calling my father what he called his own son, 'Cecil,' but my father's benevolence had its off-limits, so Alistair called my father 'Cec,' like everyone else. But he had a way of saying it that left a vacancy afterward, a vaguely foreign enunciation and then a pause that implied 'il,' and I knew he was thinking of his son, wishing the bad 'Cecil' had turned out like the good 'Cecil.'

I resented that. Alistair never acted grandfatherly toward me. Why didn't he look at me and see a little Bad Cecil running along the side of the road after a Pure Springs bottle? Bad Cecil before he turned bad? I was good. Why didn't my father brag to Alistair about me as if I were the grandson between them? Instead, all they ever talked about was Bad Cec, his early exploits with my father, his recently rumoured exploits elsewhere in our murky province. He could 'spot an undone blouse button at the opposite end of a crowded dance hall on a Saturday night with a blindfold on.'

Those wild days were supposed to be over now. My father had mellowed, at least during weekdays. Saturdays were for rye; Sundays were for 'sleeping it off.' He had forbidden the old boozehounds to come around except on New Year's Eve. Then he'd give them a shot of whiskey, and my mother would make onion sandwiches.

My uncle Fred, my dad's half-brother, came every New Year's. He'd never sit on a chair, just hunker by the door in his blue overalls. His favourite saying was 'Eatons don't tell Simpsons.' Translated into the evaporating history of my family, this meant 'Each generation is bound and determined to tell and give the next generation nothing but a hard time.'

THOSE BLACK IRISH EYES that made my mother's mother so

ugly, my mother's brother so handsome, my father so mean-striking –

the almost primate Black Irish eyes are dying out in me and my

children. (And their children …) Our eyes don't smoke nor grudge-

hold as much – more and more they beg pity, evasively, in behind.

In my mother the legacy of such eyes complemented illness, low

iron in the blood (for which she took the Little Liver Pills I thought

were to keep her liver little), a bad heart and, toward her end,

obviously too many cigarettes (the brown fingers – I'll get to fingers).

My mother's mother wasn't all that ugly, at least when young. She

had an arresting face (an arrested face). Those eyes: the valid – no-less-

magical – connection between chicken hawks and tyrannosaurs was in

those eyes of hers, and those eyes before hers – a ruthless, unforgiving,

unforgotten-by-the-nerves history of land betrayal,

disenfranchisement, starvation, exile. Not one of us remembers, but

those black eyes alert above either side of that beak of hers

remembered somehow for us all. I can see that blood-memory in early

photos of my grandmother standing with her sisters and brothers

behind their mother's chair.

ALL HER BONES bled into her mouth
to form an egg there when she died

allowed – that damp enormity smell
of crimped dirigible tripe

despite – many a starched Adam's apple
given – flabbergasted stump-puller patents

of course – the functional architecture
of animal husbandry's crude features

in any egg bequeathed to an only daughter
egg the daughter shoved up inside herself

behold in granddaughter eyes
candled china

NOT JUST IRISH: British Isles *Heinz* – the Highland Clearances meet the Potato Famine meets child mining deaths in the Midlands and the pagan Greek connections of the White Goddess near Tintern Abbey ... those eyes.

In people robbed of heroism and shunted into harsh exile such eyes looked as show-stoppingly out of place as an immense nose on an otherwise ordinary face. So much anger just sitting there unresignedly, its intensity darkening the skin of the lids, deepening the crow's feet, making the bags shine black as they sagged under. And all of this dying out, which is not necessarily so regrettable, considering how for generations the frustrated rage in such eyes would come blaring out as family violence, a tradition of disowning those who were loved most, of not speaking, ever again.

BUT FIRST
unflinching algal eyes
  drilled at the pass

at rest in attacklines
  they oiled & combed their long hair
with bone combs

  a grim reverent dawn halfhour

that unguent day
  a bone comb
their gods' only weapon
  against ruthegories

(ear-stirrup powdered
  between-toe unhouselled)

this bone comb
  dug down to / sifted for
still says *come whole to underearth*
  hordes are to core-sample

come noses arms unlopped allegiances
  of white-grained dorsal-stone
undabbable eye-trillettes &

  then they left combs stuck in their tresses
& daylong butchered the north men
  who came & came undiminished though the pass

grunting the names of more vehement gods
  who have thrived to fund this research

MY UNCLE'S EYES are still alive, the only black ones remaining. I keep meaning to go visit him, but ever since his son shot himself (he also had those eyes, in spades), I've felt awkward calling, unsure. I'd like to see if in my fingers he will recognize my mother as immediately as I do – the resignedness of the rural poor on the edge of the Canadian Shield in the ancient Fifties – my mother's sick, dark eyes watching a butt smoulder against her fingers.

Even the wrinkles at my knuckles have personality not completely my own. There is a composite character to each finger. Each nail is a blank somehow-familiar face. I could study my uncle's face and he could study my hands to avoid my weak eyes and we could both remember and wonder about his son who was named Perry after Raymond Burr, a lousy actor, like us all.

SPEARING PINEAPPLE RINGS from a can with a stick

piqued by the moment's tenacity – its appropriation of
  the wrecking yard around the epiphany

I have unfolded the road map of the axhead
  & found even in its wagon ruts & foot paths
the same devotion to flung balance – the same hierophany
  a tree displays in its cold twigs & seed tips &

unfullblown asymmetrical ornament-hammered gasket-crumbled

(Father a serial killer of pets
  Mother a falsie shielding a prone *tick*)

born joined at the head with myself – *monstre sacré*
  hurt into balladeering (take it away boys) – been verified

squat in song beneath the slide-rule bridge
  – *darkness yellow grass a blip gristle*

IN A GENERATION of men who more or less all looked (or tried to look) like Robert Mitchum, Bad Cec had the mixed blessing of looking more like a puny George Orwell. Though he wouldn't have known who Orwell was, maybe not even who Mitchum was. My father certainly looked like Mitchum (and knew it), and came to look even more like him as he and the movie star both got older and thicker.

Bad Cec never ate. He just drank. So he was all bone. He had the eyes I mean. In a person with wider features those black eyes would have been heartbreakers, but Bad Cec's face was pinched, so he looked like a bird of prey. His grey brushcut was combed harshly back so that it stood, and his pencil mustache donated vanity to the intensity in his eyes. The result was that he looked at once rivettingly interesting and suspiciously psychotic. He had a face built for a flask of straight vodka, and for women who had been abused into thinking that crude jokes were romantic.

THOSE MEN WHO DO   smear
seem devoted
   to the ice-rim-lit
muck-filled hoof-holes   caul
   bodies are

                                                    aside

fly over helpmeats
   right into couvade pretense   with
become epigrammarians

                                                    one

   horrified lest tongues of Babel
go-go above bowed heads to loosen   hand
   nooses of exactitude

they idolize & minimalize
   the rhyme of the brooch-pikes   blow
in the old king's eyes
   (gore is what Tradition likes)   snot from

MAN DIES CRUSHED BY HIS OWN ADDRESS   nostril

   or the blindman in the park
beseeching his dog *Anus! Anus!*

                                                    support

I am my own ex-wife he says

                                                    little

I am the little pyramids
   of paper caught under the staple   neck
when legal pages are torn away

                                                    with other

a glider's chewed off paw

                                                    hand

yet here comes that horizon
   he had made for himself special

plate tectonics ahem   uncherish

how a man loves a pact that stunts!   fallow

29

OR ORTHODONTICS: a class issue. The unlocked jaws of prodigals opening to the infinite mysteries of cowering self in troubled sleep. *Relax completely* – try to do like the book says – *take a tension-inventory from big toe to soft-spot* – we try to be how the books all say we can be – but a lower lip still rises to cover a snaggle-tooth. These crooked teeth: some stronghold our jaw muscles camouflage – even afraid of baring our fangs when we die – out of our depths in the shameless hordes. Old age home men butterfly-kissing death still don't want a long hair on a nose or an eye-lid snipped away. Or university lockjaw so others couldn't see our parents – our poverty – our determined shame then (shamed by that shame now). From years in the Talking Class we are almost too well-trained to open our mouths to join in abandon our own people. *Relax* – the books all say – but for centuries we could only snarl at hens' tracks read to us as Law.

THROUGH OLD BREEDING wound sleep
descend unto inner organs
                        whereupon

   sire & namesake awaken in cold fog
on islandrock milksnake-rife

   each organ a word in a story
each word a camped sight

   & no canoe off
                just this lack

WE LIVED up the 9th Concession, just about a mile north of the first defunct cord-line, and just about a mile south of where the old floating bridge sank in Devitt's swamp. The cord-line was only dysfunctional west of the 9th; east of the 9th it was about three miles to Rokeby along narrow, winding, gravel roads lined with pine stump fences. (You'd have to walk it.)

My father was a mechanic, but in the winters he used our immense black horse, Toby, to log cedar that he bought from poor farmers willing to lose their woodlands for a percentage of what Rokeby's and Jermyn's were paying. Summers, he drove a Euclid (a 'Yuke' – one of those cyclopean prehistorics) for Bob Thompson Construction. That is, he did until carbon monoxide collapsed one of his lungs. After that he fixed cars, and got rid of Toby. He built Dancey fence: props and stakes bundled with wire at the section-heads – all paid under the table, of course, so as not to interfere with his Veteran Affairs pension. A dollar twenty-five a rod is what I think he got for those fences that are still standing.

raft of squared pine / ash

   mid-porridge half-chawed
(John L. Sullivan mustaches)

   indefinite articles facing
definite articles facing back – 'the secret

   of the Particular transforming itself into the General
& of the General transforming itself into the Particular'

   (Czeslaw Milosz)
History playing Red Rover with

   the names for things – *aaas*
& *thethethes* calling each other

   over – Sirs & forgotten Givens &
mobs of Nicks trickling in along

   erudition-overpasses that lead down (& out)
to pseudo-wisdom-gulley scrims – this theatre-heat

   the a the a the athe atheatheatheatheathe
that is us as almost each other

   on a radiator the warm phone book
we are all in – peptides & amino acids –

   anonymous whirring
posed adrift

OUR PLACE was a fake-brick farmhouse that two twin brothers had lived in all their lives. It was told of these two brothers that they were so moronic as to order women out of catalogues – surprised when all that came were dresses. They chewed tobacco and spat at the box-stove with such bad aim that all around the stove was permanently gummy and brown. Every other spring they bought a new sheet of linoleum and laid it overtop. When we moved in, we tore up six or seven layers of linoleum all stuck together, board-hard, with 'baccy spit.

The land was sold at auction after their deaths to Lloyd Junkin. He was apple-flushed, balding. We rented the house from him for thirty bucks a month, and Lloyd was around once or twice a week, harvesting or pasturing the land. He wandered shoulder-deep in blue oats, pulling up mustard. He kept cows in my barn.

BOXER, TIPPY, CHICO, Sugar, Toby, Dobbin
Dobby, Mimi, DeeDee, Princess
Little Johnny Fucker-Faster, Rusty Warren, Uncle Bobby
Sweet Daddy Siki, Whipper Billy Watson
Wilf Carter, Hal Lone Pine
daddle-daddle, bullrod

I WAS IN GRADE four when we moved there. I remember my

desolation at pigeon shit on the inside window-sills upstairs. In the

barnyard there was a horse-hair-seated cutter torn by limestone

weather. There was a salt-lick in a wooden trough. It was protected

from rain by the grey roof of some car from the Twenties. Not the late

Fifties like the calendars said, not for a long, poor, rural while yet. Still

Oliver Mowat's Orange turn-of-the-century Ontario, my porkchop-

shaped province, outhouse-shaped county, shape-shifting township.

OR
      LIE DOWN in the dry tub
with the lights off
              & just sob

   each flourish a retreat
from the glare & responsibility of
   a small truth about
             the self

an earth-moving species
   modifarious underway inisolate
tracking the verb *to be*
             by its warm scat

   peeled phrases
           raw decorum
brambled innards

          tongue-tied dendrites
   hobbled strays
      the self

a species almost extinct
   before discovery
        or

A WOLF HAD COME into a barnyard and attacked a calf. The farmer surprised it and chased it off with a shovel. There was no snow on the ground yet, and deer season was still weeks away, but the air tasted of snow. The November sky: frosted tin.

My father and other local shiftless types, plus a few idle farmers, were employed by Victoria County that year in the Winter-Works Programme (a Diefenbaker Tory incentive). What they did was cut brush along the sideroads in exchange for their welfare cheques. The men on the crew had also been getting together on weekends and wet days to wolf hunt. They were impatient for deer season and snow and tracks. The wolf scare, various unreliable sightings, had thrilled them, made them keen to drink rye out-of-doors together, talk about lumber, stooks of oats, driveshafts.

Excited by the atmosphere of that November, I also went out on weekends and after school, by myself, with my gun.

And one Saturday afternoon when the shadows, to keep warm, were whipping up and down the fields, I discovered a massacre: blood and gut-slime all over a low stone-pile back near Devitt's Settlement. Surely a calf the wolves had brought down and fed on.

Breathless from running home, I had my mother call Lloyd Junkin.

WHERE WINGS ONCE caught poor sinners like us
in billowing Tennysonian mounds

a tear has sprouted a white hair
as hard as a spike but it will grow silky

if continents again tonight go to sleep turning pages

in a gathering flock that darkens the quiet
until each reader is the red-tailed hawk

on the fleur-de-lysed spire of the dance church

warily she hooks her beak into wet breast feathers
& lifts bifocals at a splinted angle biting

we put on the hoods of our stories & fly inward

we pry open & pick at what nips the crux
of wings we don't have

while the wings we foreswear for sleep shrivel stink

& the ones we have turned our backs to in bed
are plucked awake at 5 a.m. to reinforce the moats

against the spike of the white hair piercing the tear

WHEN LLOYD arrived, I led him back through his fields. Talking non-stop, I impressed upon him my woodlore and savvy.

When we got to the slaughter-site, when I stood beaming over my revelation – the red-faced farmer said, 'Afterbirth.'

And walked away.

There were many fall calves that year, many rumours of wolves. I never saw one wolf. My father's hunting crew never saw one wolf.

As they all stood drinking around a fire in the bush, I heard my father recite a poem: '*There once was an Indian Maid / Who said she wasn't afraid / To lie on her back in a cowboy shack ...*'

My cousin had told me this one too. I watched my father's mouth move until blood blocked my hearing. I saw the other men miming howls: '... *came a cowboy grunt / With his ass between his eyes*'.

JUST TO STAND ALONE in a field
was horrifying

let us have a look at you
was horrifying

the clouds had swallowed horse pills
Alfred Payson Terhune hated me

there were pin-worms in my scat
an Australia of plaster snored on my bed

holes had rabies / insects were chainsaws
even Thornton W Burgess hated me

– mirror-sapling lashing back
whiting the pulp of my khaki iris

a zigzag fence in the dolphin snow
had become a trail of stained glass shards

my father had built those fences
& now they had become Kristallnacht

a fortification-spectrum
an aura

I SAT IN THE CUTTER, plucked out horse hair and looked at the empty barnyard, the stone-piles in the fields, the pine stump fences. I felt as old as my father's dead father, as unwanted and useless as a broken plowshare.

If only Good Cec hadn't made me shoot the dog, its eyes hot stones broken open, full of cream.

That's when the dreams started. I got a fever and its dream has been with me ever since. I am little, on my back, & above me the earth in space is growing, cracking – buckled and warted – a baked apple. That earth grows until it fills my vision. I can't see its circumference anymore. Why is the earth going to sit on my little face? There is no sound. I can smell brown, sticky glue – the kind used on fly-strips. I am widening my eyes to keep the earth-apple up there. I can't – huge, crusted Earth falls on me. I am awake, screaming.

1. THE BANJO / in the canoe: sex

2. C-section / chord

3. a flat head & one arm in a banjo case
   overboard

4. drift & pick / choice meander

5. enough of 'yet not despairing' (new funtears)
      enough of 'ultimately transcends confessional'

6. as if late optimism weren't fear come up at sea
      for the third time / abloat / gangly with bio's
      godawful song

7. let groans fill the ruts in the hills
      of widening jetstream reflection be

8. broken ribs & wires awash –
      another long dockless scar

FIRST TIME THE DREAM occurred, my father came in. He wiped my forehead, not knowing this would be the only memory I have of him touching me, beyond handshakes.

If only he hadn't left the skinned carcasses of the young raccoons nailed to the woodshed wall that Sunday.

THERE ARE CHILDHOODS of table salt
childhoods of cow salt
    childhoods of no salt at all

I shared a blue lick
    with the landlord's herefords
& night deer

    our tongues wore deep scoops
in those sky blocks
    (similarly ocean glass)

others had to die to run away to sea
    I stepped away from the yard light
& gave up human pride

    for the tilt & pucker
of animal fear – am still awash
    & bitter (let it go)

(HOW I MANAGED to get 100% on my science exam by drawing

with coloured pencils the life-cycle of the frog. Filling a sheet of

foolscap with transformations. And why a warm ghost-thrill is still

activated between my shoulder-blades each time I think of that

triumph. How the exam was delayed a week because our rural school

had no foolscap. How it was spring and we reeked of wild leeks fried in

pan-lard. And the peepers were loud. And the bulls were deeper. But

who listened to that same old cautionary chorus? Rather pump my

BB-less air rifle, then wade in and shoot, up close, hard air into the wet

sky I despised in their know-it-all eyes bumping out of the algae.)

THE PLOWSHARE of the turkey's breastbone. Slick plates. Elbows of bread crust.

She stood in the dark kitchen, clutching boxes of gifts from local merchants.

Her father hadn't thought she would win.

He had told her not to be disappointed. He had said that the Shopkeepers and the Teachers would make sure the Snow Queen was one of their own.

She had left the turkey stuffed and ready in its pan. She had covered it with tin foil. All she had asked Joan to do was put the bird in the oven at 2:30. She'd be home before it had to come out.

TRAMPING THE LINE between pillows
has become a pilgrimage to a used teabag

  moist reddish-brown on the grassy tracks
how sweet *emotional incest* sounds

  to the boy whose mother lights old wounds
& blows unseeing smoke over his body

  until he gets down on his hands and knees
& bows low – an animal sniffing

  the teabag! – his Uncle Elmer (the one he takes after)
whose innards hunkered in rabbit wire

  hey now his body's only smoke – his bones
shafts of fading light through smoke

  his marrow cells – dust motes
colloidal in the smoky light

  hey already in his public garden one tree
from foliating ochre nub to furniture emporium

  in its map-thorough negligé of milk slopped on gravel
has gone over the demon-edge & back with an astrolabe

THE FIRST TIME BAD CEC came up our gravel road I was heading back from the frog-pond. I was stepping over roots through the swamp trail that ran parallel to the Concession. I had my little German 22 cradled in my arms. He didn't see me. He was puffing from the two mile walk in from the highway. He wore flip-flops, jeans and a dark turtle-neck with a suit jacket.

I paced him along the swamp. I knew who he was. All I had ever heard had prepared me to hunt Bad Cec. I had a shell in my gun, safety on. I had two more shells in my pocket.

He stopped just past the old logging draw-road, just before where the woods gave out into the last field up to our house. I was in the trees facing him. He turned toward me. He took out his penis, held it, said, 'Oh, Baby!' to the huge hemlock that shaded him, then pissed at me. I stumbled backward. He heard something. He finished and hurried on.

TO ALMOST UNDER HOME
you ride a talking horse
   who then says *kill me*

of course you refuse – you love this animal
   (if it is an animal) you owe it your life

but then an old projector
   (whirling & clattering stink-fan)
stops – its footage-wheels seize
   (handcuffed negatives)

its heatlamp burns an orange Bonanza-hole
   through the soap-bubble of Jean Seberg's head
in *Breathless*

   horses without a talking problem
have stopped stampeding – gone into the barn
   the field doesn't know from unthundered
(quiet visible fallow)

   a bright ripple yawns grey –
those are boney suckers down there
   all facing into the current

their white pouts
   have already slid through lariats
of snare-wire – poised copper demarks
   (& lifts infinitesimally)
the sagging belly's egg-tube

   you are 6 (hush-threatened)
locked in the outhouse all morning
   with one horse-fly

no palominos
  no pubic hair (just one good yank?)

unless you dismount
  & unsheath

WHEN I WALKED IN Bad Cec was there and Mom was nervously trying to be hospitable. He had asked for a toothpick and a towel. He had taken his flip-flops off because his feet were wet. (Had he pissed on them?)

Good Cec was away on construction near Barry's Bay. Did Bad Cec want Mom to call his father, Alistair, in town? No. Was it urgent? Could we help? No. Would he like to stay for supper, nothing fancy? No. He put his flip-flops back on.

He said, 'Do you get a Fuller Brush Man up here?'

Mom said, 'Yeah, but he's a talker. Stay all day if you let him. We pretend we're not home if we see him coming. The kids like those syrup-pops he sells, but. . .'

'Tell Cec I came by, OK? Tell him Cec was asking after his old twin.'

'Would you take a sandwich?'

'No. Is there anything to drink in that fridge?'

'Well — oh, you mean, well there's some potato home-brew in there that Frank Trainer brought around last summer after the Fair. You're welcome to a glass of that. It's awful. Seeds and crud. You'd like some?'

'A swig on my way out would do me. How old are you, if you don't mind my asking?'

'I'll just call Cec at his lodgings now. He'll be happy to talk with you.'

'Barry's Bay?'

'Yes.'

Then he looked at me. 'Your dad and I are best friends. Did he ever tell you about that? … Are there any bears around here?'

'Some,' I said.

'Could I call Cec for you?' Mom said.

'I'll be going. Thanks.'

'Take this potato jug along with you. Mind the sediment. o κ?'

'o κ,' and taking the bottle, he went.

It was getting dark. We watched him walking away and then Mom put *Maverick* on.

'JOAN! GET UP! Get up and get out of here! Right now!'

Her father's girlfriend rolled onto her back on the couch in the living room, made a questioning groan, half raised herself, then lay back, silent.

Her father, on the other couch, sat up, adjusting his suspenders.

'I won.'

She dropped her boxes on the floor and ran upstairs. She went into their bedroom and pulled slacks and shell-tops out of drawers. She piled bras and slips, carried an armload downstairs, kicked open the front door and threw the lot into the snow.

'You heard me. Get up and get out. What did you do to the turkey?'

Joan sat up, groped at her feet for her lighter, lit up, stared into her lap, sucked a tooth.

'Stop sucking your damn tooth and get out, I told you!' *Her father got up, went to the table, sat down. The cap of a vodka bottle spun.* 'Come here and sit down.'

'No.'

In a while he said, 'You won?'

'Yes.'

'That's good. I would have liked to see their faces.'

'What happened to the turkey?'

'Joan's kids came to see their Mom before the holiday.'

'And you let those retards eat my turkey? Look, it isn't even cooked yet.'

'It's good. Cold now, but try some. There's some left here.' He stripped a bit of turkey away from a bone, and washed it down.

Joan said, 'Is there any vodka left?'

'You get your things and get out of here. I can't stand it any more, Dad, make her go.'

'You have your friends and your presents – what do I have?'

'Oh for fuck's sake, not this again!'

'You're not too big to go over my knee, even if you are their Snow Queen.'

'Leave her alone,' Joan said, and blew smoke at the ceiling.

'Shut up, you.'

'Shut up yourself, and give me my car keys. I know where I'm not wanted.' Joan didn't get up, though.

'You're too drunk to drive,' her father said.

'It's my car,' Joan said.

'Who paid the last insurance? Who fixed the timing?'

She picked up her skates and said, 'Look, I'm going back into town.'

'You just got here.'

'I have to go back.'

'I'm sorry.'

MY SISTER had a thing for jailbirds, so there were others who walked up Concession 9. They toed the gravel, rarely looked anyone in the eye, were always dressed inappropriately for the weather. Summers, they'd have on checkered, fur-lined vests, or on their feet would be white mukluks. Winters, they'd wear pointy dress shoes and sports jackets. They declined rides; they declined food. What they wanted was never clear, especially if my sister wasn't home.

I think my father was a father-figure to them, just as Alistair was to my father. Sometimes I wished that Bad Cec was my father, because he would look right at me and teach me all the awful things he had learned how to do.

If only my cousin had kept off me, kept out of me his brown fly-strop glue, his shot dog-eye cream. Afterwards, he would comb my hair to a wet Elvis point between my eyes and warn me what his wolves would do to me, and where I'd be sent, if I ever told.

'I'M SORRY too. I just have to go back into town.'

'Do you want me to drive you?'

'I'll drive her,' said Joan. 'I can.'

'No. No thanks, Joan. Dad.'

'Is there skating tonight?'

'I think so.'

'What about supper?'

'I'll get some chips at Ming's or something.'

'Do you need money?'

'No.'

'I'm proud of you. We showed them —'

'I'm going, OK? Should I turn some lights on in here?'

'No.'

ONE YOUNG GUY kept getting thrown into Millbrook Prison for beating other guys up. Then we'd go every Sunday to Millbrook to let my sister visit him. While we waited in the car, I could hear the prisoners playing baseball. One time a ball came right over the wall and rolled to a stop on the grounds, but Good Cec wouldn't let me get out and fetch it because he said that ball was government property.

GROUNDHOG STOMACHS combusting on the lawn.

Wild leeks and morels frying in the kitchen.

Only Rage's feet visible, sticking out from under the 1956 Pontiac.

A blue spark in my head is whitening to the cutting point of an escape tool.

'Hand me that 7/8s socket wrench,' shouts Rage, whose hand appears, snatches the tool from me, curses.

I have handed Rage the wrong tool, again, and so must hightail it up my apple tree, aflame …

No, Rage is in a burning treetop, and it is Silence on its back under the leaking black and white junker.

I MET HEMINGWAY when I was 10, in hospital for a late

circumcision. ('My thing's closing up on me,' I said to my dad, when I

finally couldn't pee anymore. 'Didn't anyone show you how to clean

yourself?' said my dad.)

In the prep-arena I turned on my gurney & facing me was a naked

man with a thick, clipped mustache, Mountie-fashion. He was staring

at me & screaming & all burnt (sausage-fashion). Screaming at me as if

I had burnt him. And somehow I had.

Me, who opened a partridge's crop & emptied it of tiny stones. Me,

who fingered the plucked & cut-away breast-meat for pellets & helped

my father fry its tawny limpness in butter. Me, who toasted with a lens

a grasshopper I called my cousin.

I had flame-thrown this man up before me to scream what I was

too terrified to scream.

MY MOTHER'S AORTA misfired (rheumatic)
my father had no fear of the gods

the world is one bone & I am another
still yearning can be farmed like roses

its true shape can be found & held
though I am fear on fire that longs

to be bone-meal thrown at a breeze
into the body's gardened shiftings

will drop the soul's cameo
& somewhere someone's roselike profile

is or has been this shadow's twin
(immemorial shuffled searching)

murk-wet cord / gut-cut halo
thumb-smoke / fearfire / *feiare* –

HERE WAS ME /Hemingway inside-out, his/my war-trauma on display. I didn't hear us scream. I don't hear us scream in memory now, even when I lift into my eyes again the scab of a Nick Adams story: *the rabbit he shot had a cancerous tumour on its head.*

A nurse turned me away: I wasn't supposed to be facing in that direction, seeing my man's nude hell. But that was Hemingway, that was who I would become as man & as writer, unless.

I understand Hemingway's writings better thanks to the unreal gift of that meeting. I understand why I ate whole his shelf-section of the highschool library in an attempt to unite my father's rage with my own ambition to write my way far from that rage.

The Sixties couldn't begin until Papa blew his tortured strut off the page. Until my father died I couldn't begin grafting skin from my inner thigh onto our battlefield.

DEAR NOW LATE YOU candle light

as if you could read by candle light
   how in my dreams these days doorways
are stopped up all but for headspace
   near the floor (or transom) my shoulders
won't fit through even if I get down
   on the floor on my back & turn my thoughts
away from you so I get up & in my fury
   butcher rooms again with that little sword
you gave me then I take another bath
   not a cleansing really a long soak
two three times a day these days – rehearsing
   a re-write of caesarian birth maybe

night candled tremble y/our fear

THERE WERE CALLS late at night sometimes. Alistair would want

my father to drive him to Cobalt or somewhere. Bad Cec had gotten

himself in trouble again. He was in jail, or was sick, or he was drunk

and broke and hungry. My father would always just put his pants on

and go. No questions asked. When he returned home the next day he

never said anything about what had happened. He always was one to

talk about the sanctity of friendship, though, and I think he loved the

adventure. The dangers of driving long distances in bad weather also

always appealed to him. I never got to go, and Bad Cec never came

home with Good Cec after one of those night missions.

If only my oldest sister's two-month-old daughter, Nancy, hadn't died

while being breast-fed. Our party line rang at 2:30 a.m. – one long, two

short.

JUST BEFORE DAWN began to twist
piss-light out of its cloistered linen
    I found the fetal position again

my last upper-thought was of walking tours

    the lone righteous Pilgrim's stride
lost in doubt-extravaganzas
    down among besieged cells

I put my thumb in my mouth as of old
    & entered my shadow that straw-kneed boy
cupped in Pharaoh-sand under glass
    in the quiet dark locked museum

out from us each incubating the other
    strode little Bunyans we call *the program* now

the fearless reach of a walking staff
    poling half-red for the territories

other-may-I elsewhere ...

ALISTAIR SURVIVED on his old age pension, and he was close to 80. It became difficult for him always to be helping his son.

What happened was: Bad Cec got into big trouble. I heard 'knife fight.' I heard 'Wawa.' I heard 'drunk tank' and 'Harbour Light.' But when Bad Cec called this time his father was in Lindsay Hospital: pneumonia and a stroke.

Bad Cec called us. My father drove to Lindsay, to visit Alistair in the hospital. He told Alistair about the new problems, but the old man couldn't help. He was sick, and didn't have much money. He needed to pay the hospital.

He had sent 'Cecil' a pair of new boots only the month before, and he had put what money he could spare into one toe. They were the best boots he could find. He couldn't do any better. It was difficult for him to speak.

SHE WENT OUT into the cold, her kingdom.

A car was coming.

She tramped through Joan's clothes in the snow in the dark.

At the road, high beams caught her.

A WEEK LATER, Bad Cec came to the hospital. It was March. Ice was groaning at the lake edges, and the gutter drains were plugged with slush. It was raining wet snow. Bad Cec had his new boots on. No coat. No hat. He was very drunk. The pullover sweater he was wearing was too small for him. Underneath, a bulge along his left side – a dressing over a wound.

He needed money. Right then and there.

His father was sorry.

'You damn well have money and I know it. Where is it? I want it. I need it. You've never given a good Goddamn about me.'

'Please don't yell. The nurses. The guy in that bed over there had his prostate out yesterday.'

'I don't give – !'

'Do you like your boots? Do they fit o k?'

'Yes.'

'You need good boots in this weather.'

'What I need is $200. I owe a guy.'

'Cecil, look at me. I don't have it. I wish I did.'

'You're a fucking liar and I know it.' He had built and hoisted a grey fist.

'Did you spend all the money I put inside the boot?'

'If you like these fucking boots so much you can have the damn things back!' He sat down and was unlacing when a nurse came in.

'Please try to be more quiet, sir.'

'What has this old bastard ever given me? Nothing. I'm giving him my fucking boots, o k, so just bugger off and leave us alone, *sir*.' She left.

Bad Cec took his boots off and set them meticulously under the side tray-table. His father, protesting, could only push the call button while Bad Cec walked like a hero off the ward in his grey lumber socks (red trim), out of the hospital, into the weather.

YOU WERE ALWAYS beside him – breathing
with him in quick puffs through a green mask

sipping from his groin-eye
wet in the mirror on the ceiling

you are terrified of what hasn't come
(think of what by now it may have become)

he keeps trying his metaphormost
to show you what there is to be so afraid of

nurses – grown children – legintimates
may all be leaning over you in green masks

trying to breathe for you – & you still trying
to breathe with him

straining to help him deliver what
his freak-of-nurture self still half-believes

must be kept from those who hope to grow up
capsized courageous –

he breaks your watch with a puff of breath
you needn't be afraid of his love

EACH TIME I SEE panties along a highway, or a child's mitt in an

alley, an ominous foreboding backhands me. I imagine the ways our

clothing comes off, and am never far wrong.

And am what, to imagine us all so exposed so glaringly?

I recognize my feeling, at such moments, as the one inside my old

recurring dream: Earth explodes and falls on me as a nude bends

beside a car. A dump manager screams when a phone rings (one long,

two short). Bottles shatter.

Dog's eyes crack; wolves howl: 'Don't tell!'

The pillow Rage dreams on festers and arrives.

Good Cec takes a swig and looks away from me in disgust.

Bad Cec stumbles in his sock feet through torrents.

SHE STUCK her thumb out and smiled hard.

I AM AWAKE at 2 a.m. The phone rang, I guess. I listen to my voice, beep, then deep silence.

Skittish. Divorced twice; two kids. Sober almost two years this time. I stand nude in the dark, hiding my crooked teeth from who? Whom?

A bachelor apartment. A sore stomach. An ear infection.

'Pale, but interesting.'

Should I turn some lights on in here?

By heart I peruse my younger sister on paper on the side of the highway, her smile caught in those high-beams. The clothes in the snow beside these torturous poem-tries ...

Gulping mineral water. With a swagger not my own. Taking my lack-of-medicine like a Cecil. A grimace too sour. Too twisted. For this normal unhappiness. Tolerates only bent. Flat crowing.

Lost in the maze of talking alone.

'No child survives.'

the whole story is not *my mother*
burnt the pogey cheque or
woke us all up because she had won
the Legion jackpot ($87)

the whole story is not my father
always threatening
to disappear up lumber trails
that lead to a khaki Trenton
findable only two fingers at a time

until tracheotomy sprung him

I thought embellishment
was my flight out
when we lived in Norland in '53
he worked in Arscott's garage
but the pit grease gave him boils
& his teeth were infected

he stood in that garage doorway
with his mouth full of gasoline
until the pus in his gums broke
then he spat & quit

my mother cored the boils from his neck
with a hot jacknife but I was wrong

narrative won't solve this
piecemeal din
that is not 'archivally sound'
nor democratic

. . .

. . .

a map of the maze
    may lead to the bloody horns at its centre
& a string of anecdotes
    may get you back out a hero

but to build such amazement
    is a tower prison

from which to worship
    the twists & turns of style
that promise salvation
    but are themselves the bull

the whole story is not just mine
    to unearth by pageantry – is a multiple
common held in trust – is what
    be/longs us

errors rip like sustaining dreams
    through the chronicle fragments

(late of County Itinerary
    a $12 suit in my spleen
postmarked Skugog Island
    tomorrow we will be in ...)

& the silence between the versions
    is where the reverence holds

if I knew more
    I'd say less

A Note on the Cover

The tripod sculptures on the cover are by Richard Henriquez, the Vancouver architect and artist. They are used with his kind permission:

The Weight of a Tree (1991)
Tripod Sculpture with Cleaver and Plumb Bob (1992)
Mythical Creature with Power Shoes (1990)
Tripod Sculpture with Shoes and Wooden Eggs (1992)

From the exhibit: *Richard Henriquez et le Théâtre de la mémoire* (Centre Canadien d'Architecture, Montréal, 1993)

'Henriquez alters the tripod by separating it from the equipment it once carried, and makes something entirely new by replacing that equipment with the compositions of found objects it now supports.... These instruments that once helped to situate and define one's relative place in a measurable world, Henriquez replaces with open-ended representations, usually found objects in surprising juxtapositions.... In the architect's living room, many of the dozen or so of these sculptures (Henriquez continues to produce new ones) have a rough, unfinished quality, in fact Henriquez often rearranges their tops. Although satisfied with a few, he seems reluctant to effect closure, to lose their value as laboratory experiments where formal possibilities can be tried and discarded and from which the benefit may surface only in the built work, that is, in another context, medium, and scale.'

(Howard Shubert)

Photo: Trevor Mills

Phil Hall's first book, *Eighteen Poems*, was published in Mexico City in 1973. Since then he has published three chapbooks, a cassette of labour songs, and eight other books of poetry, four of those with Brick Books. Among his titles are: *A Minor Operation, Why I Haven't Written, Old Enemy Juice* and *The Unsaid.* His last book, a long poem, *Hearthedral: A Folk-Hermetic,* appeared from Brick in 1996. He works as an editor and a teacher and lives in Toronto.